IF THIS IS THE AGE WE END DISCOVERY

ROSEBUD BEN-ONI

ALICE JAMES BOOKS

Farmington, ME

alicejamesbooks.org

IF
THIS
IS
THE
AGE
WE
END
DISCOVERY

10 9 8 7 6 5 4 3 2 1

Alice James Books are published by Alice James Poetry Cooperative, Inc.,
an affiliate of the University of Maine at Farmington.

Alice James Books
114 Prescott Street
Farmington, ME 04938
www.alicejamesbooks.org

Library of Congress Cataloging-in-Publication Data

Names: Ben-Oni, Rosebud, author.
Title: If this is the age we end discovery / by Rosebud Ben-Oni.
Description: Farmington, ME : Alice James Books, 2021
Identifiers: LCCN 2020034004 (print) | LCCN 2020034005 (ebook)
    ISBN 9781948579155 (paperback) | ISBN 9781948579490 (epub)
Subjects: LCGFT: Poetry.
Classification: LCC PS3602.E6685 I37 2021 (print) | LCC PS3602.E6685 (ebook)
    DDC 813/.6—dc23
LC record available at https://lccn.loc.gov/2020034004
LC ebook record available at https://lccn.loc.gov/2020034005

Alice James Books gratefully acknowledges support from individual donors, private foundations, the University of
Maine at Farmington, the National Endowment for the Arts, the Amazon Literary Partnership, and the Maine Arts
Commission, an independent state agency supported by the National Endowment for the Arts.

Cover painting by Kysa Johnson

CONTENTS

{POST} :: LUDE

For the dreamers & visionaries

Hilma af Klint, Diane Chang,
Dorothy Chan,
Freeman Dyson, Hugh Everett
& Darrel Alejandro Holnes

May we always meet in the MultiWorldVerse

"We may be entering a new era in physics. An era where there are weird features in the universe that we cannot explain. An era where we have hints that we live in a multiverse that lies frustratingly beyond our reach . . ."

—DR. HARRY CLIFF

POET WRESTLING WITH THE POSSIBILITY SHE'S LIVING IN A SIMULATION

All my timelines lead to this poem.
Proof: what brought us here is all
the same horse. So I have some questions.
Which of us are the shallow wood.
What if blood is emptiness. I suspect
my own veins are rogue simulations
flitting with a new kind of heightened self-
awareness. Proof: the nurse says they are flighty
& hard to find. *Drink more water*, she sings,
pushing her own tin. What if what's within
is simulated to keep every artery compliant.
                    You know.
That whole thing *being*
as being undead
dead creeks.

                    It's also sad to think
the envy still filling us over some horse
we knew for less than a week
is simulated. Don't you feel better at least? Well,
do I have news {for you}: I suspect the horse is
also false, bogus, *feigned*. Proof: he comes running
when we do not call for him. Proof: in one timeline,
he & I are doing a lot of simulated things.
Get your mind out of the gutter.
On holidays we openly bathe

in a {manmade}

       heated spring

       —or rather: he fears the water & balances
on edge. Half the time he slips. Falls in & blips. Holds me
responsible. Resets. *Drink more water*, tweets the anti-horse
threatening to annihilate another anti-

               {horse}

          come salt

      winter, come stone

   age. So place your bets
that advanced civilizations don't always
not annihilate themselves. Woah.
Let's try this again.
Reset.

                 *

Maybe our most real timeline resides in another verb tense.

Or is hiding in new irregular superlatives. Should we ask for
   who

     whom

         whoest. Because why be skinned when you can be
skunned. Would you do the honors. My deliberateness says to trust you.
One simulation to another, am I wrong. Didn't we see *we* through
fire, windmill, heated floors. Were we not a woman waving
a white handkerchief. One if by land. Skull
& bones. Ticks in the trees & mysterious
   {reset}

        nil & :: *please.*

                 *

If nothing else,

can we not all agree

hummingbirds win Most

Fabulous Simulations.

Even if they are the secret guards,

& their tears

the anti-virus software

injecting all those broken

1s & 0s into our hearts.

& surely in one timeline they are the gods themselves ::

the superlative *whoest*

of engineers

who've made mincemeat

of asteroids & atomic

timewears.

It's too bad that all *our* timelines are inherently self-destructive.

Proof: we watch the same video of a hummingbird snoring for hours,

still sitting in the nurse's chair & not a step closer to what life,

outside of human reach, desires. I'm okay with that.

The horse is calling.

& I'm running

my hands through his mane,

unable to explain.

Where & when this comfort,
　　this crisis,
　　　took root.

How did we meet, was it *two if by sea*.

I can't remember when we did not cheat
　　life with a horse

　　　　　　:: when all timelines were

　　a real
　　& :: even field
　　in which the humming
　　　　-bird drank our blood
　　　　　straight from the creek.

I.

Is anybody there?

—*PAPERHOUSE* (1988)

POET WRESTLING WITH HER EMPIRE OF DIRT

Aba says in a blizzard, fill the bathtub.
With firewood. Aba says a leaky roof

is a blessing. Provided
the bucket. To melt

snow. With fire. We gather.
All the trees in Queens. Shake

& shiver. My axe
cannot approximate.

My axe is a plastic bottle. Filled with club

soda. I wonder
when it unfreezes,

will it explode. Aba says light
of my eyes,

where are you getting your science.

I no longer know. I used to believe
in string theory. But the field

breaks. Too many. Rules.

& you can't quantify nor quantum
even a drop of rain— everything's just

too damn big. For models that would prove. The rules. Tried & still
not true. The roof is always leaking. The bathtub is a mass

grave of trees. Aba says go outside
before it's too late. But I have. I've seen.

In a public bathroom I hide
with many other women

from a storm. The leaky roof
fills with cinders & once more.

A dead bird. One of us screams.
They all scream. When I pick him

up off the slimy floor. Pick
the maggots from his body.

Soon. I have the bathroom. To myself.
In public. I have an entire sanctuary.

Of sorts. To mourn. When I bring the dead
home. Aba tears at his clothes & covers

the mirrors. Won't let me burn
the body. Says even birds died

in the Shoah's desperate, hungry hands
days before the bodies were turned

to ash. Perhaps this bird too descends
from a lone survivor. We cry for

his mother. We cry for my grandmother.
Free up the bathtub & flood our home.

With rainwater. Float
a burning, empty pyre.

I say: Aba, this isn't what we do
either. Aba says: It's too late

to go outside. Which I do. I try.
I dig & dig.

For dirt, defying
my father.

I lose
the feeling

in my hands. In snow
that doesn't quite stick

to the ground. Night falls
& his body stays warm

under my layers
drenched. From

sleet & sweat.
I won't give

in. Birds gather around me. Dark lights
against blue cement. They wait it out.

They stay perfectly still.
Right out in the open.

My mother believes when there's thunderstorms. That's when
they come. For our lightning. To restore &. Power. Their space-
craft. It's not ours. The electricity. Lately, whenever, my nervous
system goes. Haywire. Mama says I was born during very bad.
Bad weather. & scorn. Breaking night & water. A month too
early. Or nearly. Eight weeks. She's not sure when I came
to be. Exactly. & anyway. When there's ants on the table, I

    crush them. One by one. But not spiders. Or the fireflies
    stalking me for miles. Mama believes they know. & why
    stray cats piss all over roads. & buildings. & yet I won't. Let
    her get. Rid of them. They aren't hers. I gorge. Squid. But not
    octopi. Tempting me with their otherworldly-ness. Mama
    believes every tentacle. Is alien. Though long ago that was

        disproven. By scientists. Yet isn't all vision. Limited.
        I could tell you. How longing is the only truth. How
        I'd make revelation from lightning. Insensible. & unstable.
        As you. On earth. But that's not a reason. To stay. I can't say

            just yet. Because she wants to believe. I'm hers. & I believe.
            She knows. Why there's no respect for creatures whose only
            goals are to build. & increase. Why some come marching. One
            by one. & others bid their time. To finally. Unfurl. Magnetic
            & burning. & cyclonic webbing. Over your eyes. & law. Hurrah.
            Hurrah. She very well knows why. I've stayed so long. Do you
            know you're waiting. When I grab hold. & devour. Kin. & foe.
            In a one-shot flush random. & sour.

How early. I'll go. Early,
early. Before. A whirlwind
& undergrowth. Make me
a remote. & distant, distant

{home}

ALL PALACES ARE TEMPORARY PALACES

My niece calls with questions of asteroid mining.
At six she's worried & can't tell me why.
So we talk it out. I hear there is gold, silver, platinum
On spent comets. Who would say *I do* on a stony
Asteroid? People are already getting married underwater,
The very rich driving cars on coral reefs.
& if the newest frontiers require technology
Smaller than an atom, well, now there's the pentaquark
Which is almost all quark save for one
Antiquark, & if not for the anti-
Quark, would anything, any-
Thing at all, be? What's next is never
Enough. All left to chance shrinking. My dear, dear girl
Calling on this overcast day in the spring, where sky is one long cover
Of impassivity. *Why are we here?* She's asking for the first time,
& I hear the anxiety of one who's stumbled upon a burning
Temple in the fields. We listen to each other
Breathe. I miss my train, linger on a winding staircase
In Woodside, Queens. I remember the day I discovered
This small stretch of exposed track subverting the sky & knew
I'd come home. One more day, & I will tell her this.
One more day for life on asteroids without fences or fracking,
& dreams know no deep inelastic scattering. Let it be
Where silence is never summoned, where rays
Collide in charm & strange.

POET WRESTLING WITH EVERY NIGHT SHE'D CRUCIFY HERSELF

Aba doesn't talk about his childhood much. Or the little girl. It's Mama.
Who tells me about her. That they played together. On Shabbat. After.
His father died. & Safta had to work. Two jobs & would take. No help
from anyone. Mama's never asked. If that household kept the Sabbath.
Or what they believed. Mama showing rare restraint. Until it was discovered.
She contracted. Polio. & Safta burned his clothes. & she burned what little.
Toys they. Shared. & her own. Pantyhose. Even those the little one hadn't torn.
& grabbed. For balance. But still my father. Was exposed. & suffered. His eyes, his
spine. A whole host. *She died*. I'm told. Mama's breath. Hot on my skin. She's rubbing
around the sting. In my neck. That burns. & fades. To numbness. Along arm. &
shoulder. I'm a little numb these days. On my left side. It's not metaphorical. It's not

       political. Or related. Though I wish. Perhaps, another.
       Life. *She died*. & she. Holds me. My mother. Closer, pushing.
       Down. Where I can't really. Feel. *You have to be strong*. & it's when.
       She pulls away. I feel the blood. Running. From sharp. Sharp. Nails.

POET WRESTLING WITH AN ODE TO HER BROTHER

—After The Cranberries

I never made it through a single night.
It wasn't without design. The *brxght*.
Brxght xyxs. & still the border. Night.
    Unfurls.

        :: & the xyxs ::

        shudder through hurricane season.
          How soon. You outgrew

              as if they'd never come for you

                {standing there}

sleeping soundless

        :: without moonlight ::

          in Abuelo's three-room
          house. Still our family

                {when I was not there}

scavenges for what they left
        among weather-torn amazons
          & frond of beheaded

palm trees & raving
                        electrical wire.

Understand what I'd become:

fire in the sky & a matter of time
            illuminating the overcast
                        within faded sundress & melted

pin-feathered flesh.
It wasn't my design.
The splints for wings
            & tweezed.

                        Barb & hook

            so sure of their own goodness.

            I was so sure of their goodness & their *brxght*.
            I staked a life   {*don't turn away from me*}
                        out there

years later in Jerusalem. Until I fled. Never
was it my design. Where there's no road & no

-where left to ease. & you could not find me

                        :: {*you could not find me*}

when holding us. Over the cold floor of shul.
Saying my name until I returned. As something.
Else. Only you. Dared. My *xyxs*. &. Unhappiness

                    didn't give a damn

                              {*when I was not there*}

& you spent half your life. Bringing me back.
From out there   &

                    :: now you ask if anyone ::

                              sees you? Does anyone care? Who
                              now will scavenge & who will dare

                                        those *electromagno*
                                        & strange *xyxs*—

                              where hurricane. Season.
                              Lasts. For years. Their toll.
                              On every home. & temple.
                              Ripping through family

                    :: *& prayer* ::

Does anyone care? Does

:: anyone ::

even when I was never.
There. You brought me.
Back. Even when I've gone

back over there   —

Rest, now,
my brother.

Though my thin.
Shoulders stretch.
& bend. Haywire.
& Rusted.
& Shrugged.
Of all.
Or most.
Other.
Cares.

Rest, precious
one.

& if you turn
away {*from my brxght
xyx*} understand

::

You never had to become.
Who you are. It was always.
There.

POET WRESTLING WITH HAPPY LITTLE CLOUDS

—After Bob Ross

We tried to make our cities last a while. By beating
the devil from our brushes. & highways.   B

creates programs & code.   The kind that makes strangers
see. The little distant trees {as}. Living. Far back in the distance.

B tries to make things. Better. He tries to fix. He tries.   To realize.
Other people's intentions.   When I was with him. I felt I could make a city.

Forever. & serene. As wet-on-wet painting. That takes centuries. To dry. & realize.   Orange
-stone. Façade. Steel. Interstates. A little pink. In the sky. The rest, all little Xs.   Glimpsed

          {from bullet}

trains. Yet think. On such a world, high-speed & purely. Civil.   How we'd put in so much detail
passing everything. So quickly. From too far away. A world so advanced it's only. Form, shape, basic

          color.   We tried, he. & I. Making our city last longer.   As a way. To explain.
          Away. Why we left. Nature. Only to return. As otherworldly. & traitors.   I'm sorry

               {& foully,}

fluffy little escapes. B always has a plan.   Since I never did. Since I'm more
like you, errant & in the moment & quite often oblivious   of specific well-

being. Since when I write I'm ripping apart & shedding.   From unorthodox
brushes. & little string clouds that live. Right. In those highways. Here I can do

anything that I want to, any old thing.   But B.   Tried to make. His cities.
Where still water is always level. While I. Whatever any illusion you want. & I don't

know where any of you go—it doesn't matter.   Maybe a city is a thing already
dying.   Until naked. As a bunch of skeletons & rotten wiring.   Hanging out

here in your eyes—but even then, B would still believe. Who I will be. As who

     I was. When.

Tomorrow,   as sure as a row
of gravestone. & maybe I'll fall

too. Like what was done to you,

        {made} *acid*

& sulfuric, wearing down all that came from
what you grew,   what we can only hammer

    & chisel & scribble

unto. Such desperate, desperate.
Love. Who knows then just what

      & how I too
      will erode.

              The very good words meant

to summon a me. After you.

How we will cleave. A few. 1s

          & 0s

                        {tap, tap}

             falling

on bared knee

POET WRESTLING WITH THE DAY THE SUN STOOD STILL IN COLD NOVEMBER RAIN

Your sons fight the rain. Again. With their fists &. Swift.
Side. Kick. Again. Like most stories about conflict, I'm not
sure how it begins. Which time my mother kicked me. Out
of the house. Was it after prom or decades later, just before
the wedding? B calling from a runway in Chicago, having

made his connection. By an extra breath of a delay.
Due to unforeseeable. Rain. But the narrow sidewalk in South
Texas was dry & hot as I waited for you to pick me up. *When I arrive,*
B. In my ear. Running. Out of time. Do we *fly back immediately to New York or*
I'll never forgive myself. Hysterical. & shrill. In the passenger seat, in front
of your sons. One hand firm on the wheel, the other. Wiping my face, you
didn't need a reason. This time: my uncle was dying & Mama couldn't
find anyone else. To blame. In high school, you & I. Tried to cheat

what we were given. Of time. We belonged nowhere. Two weird.
& restless girls who cut school. To go to the one museum. Where no
exhibits ever changed. But save. The lovely, empty garden. Too small.
To wander. We talked about leaving this place. & I did. Or rather: I fled.
While you. Grew new life. Into it. Even when stuck in a quarry. Or swimming.
Up a waterfall. Trying to get home. In Minecraft. Your sons showed me how. To

scour. For minerals. Iron. Specifically. With pixelated map & unclear path.
Home. They showed me. In their way. How you reap. Dust. From concrete.
You gave. & gave. I'll never forgive myself. All the days. I took refuge in the
homes of you. & you & your husband. As fire trucks blared past. When

lightning. Struck the next house. & followed. Fires &. Untold. Damage. How a home can become unlivable. Without fighting. The rain. I think how rare.

& easy. Is such repeated. Welcoming. That night, B landed safely. We slept. Safe. & warm. In your home. The next day, my mother still wouldn't forgive me. For years of things. I had. & hadn't. Done. Should I. Should I have said. Even when I'm gone. Isn't it. Like fighting the rain. As close to you. As blood.

ALL THAT IS AND IS NOT NUCLEAR IS OUR FAMILY

I highly recommend disconnecting.

I realize the strangeness of telling you over a connection.

But here comes and goes, so I have to send things when it's working.

Things are a little rough.

In cities I am everywhere.

I don't get lonely. I lose faith that how things are

Are also how things will always be. In forever uphill rising

Streets I have a calling. She calls me from her high-rise

Office at the World Bank to warn me after ten years of *this*,

She's leaving Hong Kong—leaving *the country*—

For the week her in-laws visit.

You tell me that woman is not blood

Which means she should have nothing to say

About your family. This is not to say you

Do not treat me well. You humor me

At the chichi dim sum place

Hidden away like a speakeasy. You eat everything

I order. Often I get a pass others do not. If I have too much

To drink, you say my best thing

Is one face, not two. This is not about saving face.

We get it all out in the open, you & I.

We aren't the kind to get lonely

When we fight. You say I can't help but look like things meant

To keep you in line. You say I always take your wife's side.

We are not bad people. We understand the difference.

Difference is flickering neon until the other loses sight.

Now I'm writing this on the rooftop in a little room

You built without permission, next to a washroom

You built to make me more comfortable. Early this morning

You squeezed through the crowds at the bakeshop

To bring me a red bean bun, right out of the oven.

You remind me fish is only fresh when alive

& gasping. On the rooftop, wild cockatoos

Eat the chichi seed I recommended to you.

You never make it in time to see them.

I want to be a good daughter to you.

But then my mind wanders & Icelandic horses

Disperse through Hong Kong skyline where blood-or-not nieces

& nephews clear out of their six-days-a-week offices.

Poetry, you say, is the furthest, furthest thing from you.

What long lines, where & why they break

You won't see. Here I have no grievances. I still see the island

In this city, & you correct me: *autonomous territory*.

Autonomy, we agree, is never real in full nor fully

Realized. I say it's like coming to know a new

Father. You say one day you want to be yourself

Around me. I say once in cities I was everywhere but here

I write to you in a little room while you make your deliveries.

Dinner tonight at your favorite Vietnamese place

& then shopping in a night market. Only your son

Would chose such neutral territory.

I study the map to Ladies Market, chart the longest route.

Because you ask me to lead. Because you say nothing

When I take the wrong street. I never ask for help.

You never say we are lost.

THE SONGS WE KNOW NOT TO TALK OVER

After a funeral, something wrestles from the wind,

Flutters haphazardly close to your aching chest.

Most likely it will fall to the cracked sidewalk.

Stop walking. Consider it. You won't understand

What you are looking at, this sort of green would-be

Katydid with dragonfly wings & limbs like a praying

Mantis. It's incapable of anything

But beginning. It won't sense your grief

For someone it has been. Walk away first.

You won't see it again. Because now it's a bird.

Not very scientific, but I have seen this. Not the transformation,

But how often have I asked the sky

What comes after death & then two birds

Pass over my head. I couldn't tell you why

I awaken at times to a pecking

At my eyes. I don't know why some birds return

To haunt us. I have felt thin, small talons

Dig into my wrist. We tangle in the darkness,

Porous as loess. No trail of marigolds & copal incense.

No falconers in the boot hills. Where we go, I feel still

But never remember. In the morning a sparrow steals

A half-eaten donut from a pack of feral cats,

& I promise to spare the life of all that is winged.

I watch where I step & still a wasp stings.

I'm sorry. The only promises I've kept are those

Scientifically proven. I have no ion-infrared

Evidence, no delicate microphones to catch

When I check the closets & drains

During a thunderstorm, when I've said,

Sitting at a deathbed, it's gonna be okay.

I've told them not to pull the plug

Even if my body says when

Bury me standing, bury me

Three times. No one really drops dead from seeing

Your gaunt, flitting shape in the mirror.

Not mirror but grace. Forgive me for covering

My eyes, for cowering under the blanket, for swatting

At you when I passed a flower garden,

When I shut my windows & chased you

From park benches & fruit trees. I didn't know

There are people I'm not willing to ever let go,

& I won't. I haven't.

POET WRESTLING IN THE LAND OF A THOUSAND DANCES

You speak of future misunderstandings. I did not
let go. *See*, you text me. Meaning. *Sí.* & the door

of your childhood home does not lock. Or
fully close.   Full ditches of water & water

buffalo.   Never feasted on shrimp in this overseas
village still called *Shrimp Lair*. You ask if I could see

life in the countryside, where everybody *has gone & goes*
from.   A man strangles a goose

& then lets it go.   He's one of the few *left behind*, you say, when I take
gasping bird into my arms. Knowing injury. Is what we share. At dinner

      we pick the bones
           with our teeth & still.
                I plead for its life. *Sí*, bent.
                    Waiting. Like the *see* I thieve
           'd from my mama. Meaning she always thought me. Too soft.

For the little cumulative. Griefs.
      Same loll, same breach. When I don't.
           Stop. Crunching on the bones.
              I can't stop crunching
                  on the bones & you
                      hum along, distantly pleased.

*

Back in Hong Kong, you'll ask if the translation *holds*
up. If shrimps can live in *lairs*.　　　I think: batman,

batcave & what loneliness.　　It must be.
Wearing a mask in good faith. How true.

Grace　is a vigilante.
You'll say you starved.

Because of revolutionaries. You'll say there are no bats in your village & no city.
In the countryside. & no one stays. Up at night. Watching over. You. Say. We

　　　could renovate your childhood

home & your son & I.　　Could have a temporary
place. To escape. But no wifi　　　　& no lights

across the dirt road. At night, we'd be just us, just.
Family.　　　　　　I never lose

　　　the music. In Hong Kong.

　　Where you still secretly smoke
　　　in the tiny bathroom
　　　　when I come to visit. With your son.

　　With our eyes closed. There, the pack hidden
　　　in your robe. Like next time. Your lighter
　　　　falls out & I still pretend.
　　　　　Not to see.

You say not enough.　　　People live in the town nearby,
the kind who shop during working hours. It's a large mall,

with a spacious outdoor food court.　　All its tables clean
& empty. You say workers' breaks here are non-negotiable

& once while traveling for work you slept on a table.
Next to a man. You'd just met. Couldn't　　fall asleep.

Hong Kong has made you soft, you say.　　　Your son & wife volunteer
to find the car we'd rented. Just outside Shenzhen's rail station. At least

twice a month you make this journey. By MTR & taking. Buses. Or hitch-
hiking. You say it's too dangerous. You say the mall is all for show & here.

Is where we'd shop if we moved to the countryside.
As family.　　Today, your cigarettes are in your left

coat pocket & I know. You'd wanted me to go with them,
so you could have a smoke.　　But your son wants us to be

father & daughter.　　Like father & daughter. We pull each
other in opposite directions though we were told to stay put.

The air is grey. & osseous. Sheds soft down. My eyes water.
Our hands unsteady. For different reasons. We buy chestnuts.

You try to haggle the man down.　　Not wanting him to think you
A Hong Konger new. To these parts. You say you only have 10 yuan

when he wants 20 & suddenly.   You call to a woman across the street.
& she screams. Back at you. Today I won't see.   Why. You won't

smoke. In front of me. But later. The secrets I thought. I kept steady.
Crunching femurs & chewing organ. & sinew. The tall heels & shift

dresses & long work hours. I keep. Old photos I showed you. Of me. Scrambling
boulders & lifting. My niece. High into the air. As if it were all. Artillery. To keep

you. From seeing. How my grasp of things. Has weakened. Why we.   Can't ever live
far, far. Year-around. Like forever. In the countryside. The lack of feeling. & chronic pain

    I won't. Let win.   By being.
    Seen.   Later, as we peel

chestnuts, you explain.   You lied to the man.
You only had 10. Since your wife took your wallet.

& when the man gazed upon me, you wanted

no misunderstanding.   & so you called to the woman. Crossing the road.
Hey, give me my money! And she'd returned: *What? Leave me alone!* & you turned

to the man & said: *See? You get it.* See? Our left hands are shaking. For their
different reasons.   We huddle in the rain & wait for the car. As you text

your son. *Are you ready. To go home.* You say. Drizzle hangs.
In my eyes. It's only. A little rain. It means *sí*. It means *see*.

II.

Someone's coming
from the other world.

Hiss of night rain.

Someone's going there now.
The two are sure to meet.

— KO UN

IF THIS IS THE AGE WE END DISCOVERY

I'm never looking right when the first snow falls.

My view outside the window is broken by the fire escape.

Like most it looks rusted, painted over too many times.

This is how I must look inside.

In the hospital they have to use the smallest needles.

My veins are narrow, closed, won't let them drink

& I'm punctured so many times, I pass out.

I've come to faint days before I know blood will be drawn.

When I hear the sleet, the whipping

Of time petrified on sheetrock, I collapse

Into vessels they can't find yet

Again. As if there's no more originality,

Only riff

& mutation.

I count to ten,

As another storm snows us in

& there's nothing we could do

But fear the end. Those days too

We think are gone. We shouldn't.

If only I could say I slept. I've forgotten

When I wasn't in hospital beds & the nurses unknowing

The grace of it all

As they stroke my head: *She's gone out again.*

If only I'd gone somewhere.

If only this was to board a sinking ship

& cradled in night.

If only drowning could bring to life
This flattening world
Of black & white.

POET WRESTLING WITH *RICK AND MORTY* BUT MOSTLY RICK

It's all about the heart they say—that cross, that shine
to compromise. Either you are creator or you die

on some pagan holiday. Most everything we get
twisted. Most everything is either science or shockwave

of endless favor. The *asking*. The *ridic*ulous heart getting lit

on blood that never dries on marked doors
of unrequited sin. *Who do you think you are.* I've wed

my own body vermillion.
Blushing & brickish electric-

      plush,

these organs. Make my spleen a shrine
to excess. Who doesn't have time

for infinite timelines? Is not your greatest fear
unity, that horse I am eternally

breaking? *Is that a new dress?* Try the heart
you left

      to grey & shiver in crawl

-space,
                    {false heart} floating through

failing body. Same heart spoiling

                other hearts sulfuric &
                    weed-whack.

                        How they beat

beneath the changing of horses. Either love yourself or trust

a woman who changes doorposts & signs to unidentified

            equine.

                    Either *are* or

return to sender. You say the aim of being
you *is* {*being you*} & creation alone {is the favor}—

when all language will always escape & betray

its creator. You don't know what you are saying
of infinite pain. *Please help me.* Either horses change

to natural disasters or frozen ground heeds

the silence of its ruins. Now it's time to walk.

                        Wipe your face

            off with pure glycerin

& sage.

Creation is a spell

of double negation.

POET WRESTLING WITH HER OWN ALONENESS IN ITS TIME OF NEED {*SHE'S GOING THE DISTANCE*}

One day, soon, there will be no more science fiction. One
day. Everything we imagine. Is real ·

                though not. Everything is

a storm gathering
       in the middle of nowhere, it
            just feels like I. Can't say
                        I don't. Worry

      about the state of imagination.

I crisscross & wrestle my way toward overwhelmed airplane,

& I worry   about the states of our imaginations

        which is to say, I'm trying
          & striving
            & hugging

invisible turns
                when I worry

airport security   who's turning
      on my laptop & telling me I'm random
        -ly selected for additional

            screening,   which means I worry

you. The same TSA agent who's asking yet.
Again. What I was doing in the Middle East

over. A decade ago. You ask as if we. -'ve never met

yet know my whole. History. I want to believe. Everything.
Is real. After all. & is that   the trade-off. The residual.

Cost. For understanding {what we say. Is} human.

History I worry. We remember only. To use what we can
against each. Other.   .   & I worry, greatly,

what would happen. In an airport if I just didn't   wait

        anymore. To go off
                        course

     with the vampire bunny   hidden in my carry-on,

            yes,   a most vampiric & life-munching

             I'm carrying   even if he's mostly tachyons

          with fangs of squarks

    & smuons
                all of which decay

    too quickly
    in super

-symmetry,
all of which violate

your laws of everything
that's allowed to be

    real.   But you'll never find him, my TSA.

Darling. Who's still holding me. By the arm as if. Worried.
Who's the one *really*   on the run.   & who will approach.

          Agency.

In this small airport on the border
      where you claim. The only flight. Was cancelled
            due. To storms. Somewhere, beyond. Control.

Somewhere, a connection I have. To make.
& I'm tired of waiting for you. To give

    clearance   to the eye of my immortal

           beloved

               who waits for no one, my little, crazed & bloodless
                 fury   with too many sleptons {& too much

          heart*sick*}   churning

               & burning

in the middle of nowhere

with electrolepus caress,

on gravirabbit course,

how we defy

everything you once were

in monster-bunny force.

POET WRESTLING WITH BUNNICULA IN THE CHALLENGER DEEP

Deep sea will be the last place without borders. If they
have their way. Will never find. Or name. Most life. Here

      has no eyes or ears.
      & no pleasures they

claim. More men have floated. Through outer space. Than
four leagues beneath. They claim. Everything. Is their death

      -trap. Exclusively. & tense. & sinking.

      But we know ways beyond. Our
      tunnels aquatic. Coming. Undone.

      Oh wet & sweet. Vampire bunny.
      They'll never grasp. Hold or sour

on little bunny-powered. Nautilus. Tearing through blue
& luminous. & vamping. In bunny darkness. How bare skin

thirsts through neoprene. Is how you breathe me.
& freely. Is it possible. To explode without

      moving? The lovely spite
      of nitrogen. For oxygen.

         & what building

pressure does to chemistry.
Altering what a body. Can

take. Breaking my neck without even. Biting. How little
they know us, my salty. Vampire bunny. & our dwelling

breathless. & unseen.
Entwining on ocean floor

where they think all there's to suck
are rotting whale bones. & molten
core. Unreached. Is what presses

my neck. To your teeth. Without taking. Further & deftly.

What I could give, tightly. & at such. Depths. How we get

each other. To come. For. & Against.

We come. Without moving. We come
as the only thing
unmoving

at the bottom of the sea.

Untouched.

&. Undiscovered.

It's amazing how we won't let each other die silently.
If there is no death {then I'd rather die}. I'd rather die.
Then. I'm in love with you. Air never sleeps. The air
dies infinite

      {-ly}   alive. & the closest we come to the bottom
                          is a looking glass

we dream {inside}. Looking upon ourself—
vanishes. Can't have. Reflection. Or second.
      Reflexes. Zero {of us} is dead
          ringer. Zero is always greedier.
              When others try {to enter}, they don't *death*. But.
                  {Are. Could. Never.} Only we :: constant, constantly. & un-

ruly. By our own numbers. Zero is hunting for patterns. To the power of. Zero. Is the air erupting
    & dying while sleep,   a billion
          explosions before our eye. You're in love {with} me. & space.
              Will not empty. Voids are luscious & we're looking. Hard. Like light
                  -years of tongue. Sense thinks. *Can. Will.*
                    Separate us. Nothing, after all.
                      Is. Our language.

I don't need words,
          even these.   Only to slip into your apothecaries
          that blur fine dust into bunnies. I'm in love with the bunnies.
          Falling apart. & through. The whispering. Our eye. The screen
          freezes. & dry heave. Zero of us seeps through. Zero receives.

Static. Stasis. Lost goes. A grace. Note.

{As if two. Love would rather die you}

This kindling, wet & fecund. I don't want. To. The power of.
This groove. The air is fleeced. Zero is *swag*. Zero is {swag}.
& hungers {*I & you*}. It's amazing. How zero finds each other.
There was never a rabbit hole {& that's where zero we}.
& forget. Would rather {then}. Our lung didn't need.
Breath. Or dying. We don't {when you sing}

> *Come {back} to me*
> I'd rather die
> like the first time
> we broke free

(EFES)

"Zero"

Radla

The Highest Head,
The Unknowable Head

(AYIN)

16th Letter

Value = 70

"Nothingness"

(TOHU)

"Chaos"

III.

Efes:

(1) Modern Hebrew for "zero"

::

(2) In mystical Jewish texts: "to nullify, to conceal"

::

(3) Poet's proposal: responsible for Dark Energy, vampire bunnies & insomnia; insatiable lover; enemy of mathematics & elegant equations; Creation's Twin; presents *Nullification* properties as possible *Transformation* (rather than destruction) of the quantum & the "real" worlds; reveals Itself at the singularity of a black hole; does not abide by any law; changes the riddle

POET WRESTLING WITH THE POSSIBILITY SHE'S LIVING IN A SIMULATION {INSIDE A SIMULATION}

Consider this a death & listen. In the showers we strip naked

{until there's zero}. Gravity. & no stress but.

Its jaws. Are straining. Our necks. *Consider this*

bloodsucking. Alien. We can't.
See. Buffering. *You're lying.* On
top. Coming off. Our leash.

Mount. Moving. Neither of us. Can prove. A chance. Of relief. *Run.* Blood.
Thick. Boom. Bunnies. Extreme. Raging on the flame. As {*flames*}. Through

trees. Planets. Boreworms. Rings. How are there so few left as there are. So
many. I'm counting. High. Scores. Unbuttoning. & turning {extra}. Lives.
Into yours. Into a number taken. At a deli. Slicing off. An extra hour. That loses.
Its honey. Glazed. Rabbit. Meat moves in. On me. With sloping axe. & forest heat

{*turning*} glassy

eyes of smoked herring. Buckles the knees. Let's get real about
this. *Real is a disease.* I left hours ago. A rabid animal is not so
bold. As a force with bones to grind. {& diseases that hide.} In
brains. Stuffed. & fur-lined. Could be. Hex or. Hatbox. Real is
taking a single train. Out of service. Out of control. The inferno

is really. A dot-matrix or dial-up. That exploded. Long ago.
We jeer at those. Still holding on. To joy. Stick. & control. Extinct.
& floppy. Eared-ones that still live & lean into. Ray tube. Ray
guns. & neck cradling each one. We think. We aren't

{cassettes}

loading. Long, long ago. Our legends. Never shone. But trickled
off. Zero. Ticked. Against. A leg. Like a death. Sentence. Consider
this &. Listen. You were saying — *I love you* — More than. Just as.
Falling. Low-res. Do you wish to save. Your progress. *What miracle.*

You snap. Hard. My neck. Pixelated. Lock. Screen. Our clothes
wet as *skunned*. Animals. & dripping.

Will leave.

No off.

Spring.

{Still. In my ear.}   Hold. *God.*

God Yes. Somewhere

this is happening

without intent
or making veins.
Of tails. Somewhere

{*unnamed*

& most} incapable.

Of dying.

{Somewhere.} Never. Somatic. Only.

Heat.

& Edges.

Wetter

{*somewhere*} ::

Gravity is a grave. That will win. Its. Hunting.

POET WRESTLING WITH DERELICT SPACECRAFT

—After Gematria

Before one what do you count. The crown
is three heads & one

      is Nothingness, but nothing

-ness is not without kin. Of *Efes* & Chaos.
Efes is the tower among {Your eyes upon}

them. & I'll never find. What single limit
is driving us all apart {my *liftoff*}. Is still. My

mission reaching {for} *Efes*. & the limit exits. & I diverge
{*with eyes dripping*} from Your breath. & unspeakable

what I want
                :: *concealment*^{*of Efes*} ::
                           {in plain sight}
                                      my lips unchosen

for exodus {*still tripping upon Your breath*} what every Hebrew letter fails.
To express {this other}. Possibility. Of *Efes*. If. *Everything* is held in Your

breath. My name & known. Decay. Only. Ten. Stones. Etched. Upon like
lover. Are forever. Your hard, divine rule. Keeps me. From the event horizon

      {of *Efes*}

's gleam. When I'm free. -wheeling toward. The breath of *Efes*. When I'm. One-
thousand-second pulsar singeing. Your heavens.   Singing it will.   *Break me,*

                  Undoing.

& leave no trace. Adonai. What world. Is not Yours. {*Forgive* these eyes upon *Efes*}. This rust.
& tender. Seeking other extinct & wanton. Formations. Of contact. Contained in singularity.

Comes down to a crown. Of one. Where *Efes* is
Not shame-dreamed. Nor soft landings & burning

up in fevered atmosphere. *Efes.* When I crash

:: reentry & sight upon. Greedy & seeking threes.
Of gain. When secretes me {*through nullification*}

& spins entire kingdoms. Out of orbit & eternity.

                                        Say when I'm no longer Yours,

        Come.   {*Come*} back

    to me,   {*surrender no name*

            for all of Efes}   Lover,

                    ringing Your boson of crowns

                                                across Nothingness & Chaos,

                                        the three of Us

                    trembling like {*gutted*}

like ten broken

& tolling

  stone   rings.

{ALL I WANTED WAS EVERYTHING}

You say you know the reason why Archimedes died

tracing circles in the sand & how

you'll go out this way,

a man too in love

with unifying

theorem

& consequence.

You say you'd stake your life

in trying to understand

why gravity, like me, crushes

& slips

through your hands,

when I'm one hundred percent

certain that we are two

points never to meet,

if you keep

trying to connect the small & large of you

& me. I could tell you why Archimedes denied

the invading hand

of a Roman solider reaching out to him,

that one last chance

to surrender

& walk behind

a new empire, as free

prisoner. I could say why a frail

thing, like gravity, must be capable

of such cruelty.

I'm putting it out there,

for you,

the human body,

as a transitory stage

for what you & I will never see.

Just billions & billions of caterpillars

or maggots

or grubs,

thinking we are life's final & finite

destiny—thinking it's enough that we give

live birth & bury

our dead.   & I could say

one of our greatest was only digging

his own grave

because life taught him

nothing in the end. But my dear

friend, the science of survival is not a science

of discovery. & when we die, we go in

mystery.

{TO ZERO, WITH STRANGE LOVE}

Loving you has turned me into a given tree.
My branches are full of every warhorse, hallelujah, allegory.

When I reach for you, I count my own rings of dust
& debris. Soon I'll be a lonely stump, a last comfort

for a jilted bride, or—if I'm lucky, a resting potential
in which the last of my kind will seek rot as root.

How time lives in fear of you. My origins grow
indifferent to my deaths. & just as nebulous.

           Did I ever mean anything? Say, why

                             {in the what of you}

               are all my neurons like a plague,
                swarming you, in great numbers,

&. Vanish. Loving you means I'll never bear. Witness.

      Yet. Having a taste. Of creation. Gives. Way

           to weaknesses.   I know.

                           Only the strange radiation of a string quartet

can escape you

& when you're just about done with me

when there's just a little left   indefinite

& incomplete   when nearly *never-ment*

& so close & not unlike that

perfectperfect

{*xxxxxxx———*}

I'll collapse your veiled

{*& throbbing*}

battlements

nothing can strike at nothing
like the vibrato of cello
& violin I'll be
whispering
& holding
you   {*down*}

                    in every

                note my

            prince

    if only to tighten & twist   gulf & pit
    tune my own strings
    just to make you my fields   my fields again
    full of quantum
    wildness   {lit}
    with gamma &
              dissonance
    piercing
    through
    why not
    wouldn't we not
    be a cool bloom
    the sweetest of sweet
    nothings

POET WRESTLING WITH GRAVITON AS {{ :: *GRAVITRON* :: }}

I created you {*exo*}. From origins {*tender*} & unproven. For you.

    I crossed the streams & struck. Incurable. Fire

        left ::

           unguarded

& {untendered} desire. For you alone. I swallowed.

    Organic mercury. Nitro. Unripened.

      Neutron. Stars. I burst. & bled.

        A people. From your exo-particle.

          Veins. & vessels. Fallen. Of faithful

     .   ::

                               exodus.

                     No one can {ever} leave

               behind. Memory. Is not survival.

            But a shrill {exotoxin}. Veil &. Cry.

        {*of desperate moons*}

Spinning. Into darkness.

    & I tell myself I'm indelicate planet.

      Who'd rather hydrogen bomb

        the :: *exordium* :: of my own

          canon. Unlike you. My son. My

                          {!{ :: *Gravitron* :: }!}

I changed

one thing. From original quantum. & won't say

its name. Since the exoteric makes. Exotica

& creates both the snake. & the garden.

My sweet. Havoc. Of harbors.

Expose this.

World ::

as coded & skin-deep.

From the other side

:: {*of the screen*} ::

they so sorely want

to breach

when nothing can hold

their {*bonfires &*} fields

:: {*within me*} ::

when I'm the last I'll get it

the worst it's nothing

{*I didn't foresee*}

just so you could leave my loving

seams a little better

off a little

less

{:: *xo* ::}

POET WRESTLING WITH NEUTRINOS
SHE {ALLEGEDLY} CANNOT FEEL

We forget the body can become a way out
of life :: & death :: & you

came to a dead river across two islands with all the weight
of a wake unprepared.

Shunned, even, of wreath & rage. Nothing would grow if you didn't
have an answer

that my life was safe. I wasn't asking for your hands. Nor were it
chance if you were

to join me in collecting all the little neutrinos we aren't
supposed to feel.

But the nature of accidents isn't accidental, my friend,

in that what you think isn't there

knows exactly what it's doing

      to us
      & how
      & when.
      & what cross-

roads bear. The weight of such a question divides us

because conviction itself cannot be measured. I wasn't

>   asking for your hands— my body
>   is not two swans lost
>   to red tide :: the waves we make
>   elegiac.

It was a matter of invitation, if I should fall for it,

completely, a force greater than any strong, electro-

magnetic or weak. A force much. {*Much*} greater than

gravity. *Efes* bears the crown & brings me to my knees.

>   While it is numbers, shaky
>   & uncertain, that bind us
>   together.

>   & {*I have no*
>   *burdens only*} singing little
>   threads that bear no resemblance

to actual strings, much less two figures who can't seem

to reach each other in the shortest of distance.

They are not elegant.

I mean. My vibrations, my math. In particular.

The math holding me together is particularly faulty.

My math is *purely* strings & ^{exponentially} misbehaving.

> I am made up of much fucking {& many}
> weird equations
> full
> of anomalies

where X equals all sorts of subatomic roads

unrelated & quarreling. My {most *unnetural*} apologies.

Because it seems, no matter what, anyway, all lead

> :: back to *Efes* ::

> & do you regret watching me

> go through this

> :: {*flitting*} shape of being ::

> where gravity cannot compete.
> & rivers in which you seek
> assurances will die
> when there is no life

> :: {*left*} ::

> at poetic feet.

> When those shallow waters are stripped
> of meter, syllable & accent—only then
> will time reveal itself

:: to no one ::

                                    that it is nothing

compared to a force living
outside of it.

I'd be lying if I said I didn't fear *Efes*

        as much as I murmur & hiss
        against all these little strings
        having their way with me.

& I'd be lying if I said I didn't

        *:: like getting heavy *heavy* ::*

                with all these bomb solar neutrinos,

                        the *wild-on* ghost particles
                        seeping into my body
                        when they shouldn't

                        affect me, much less
                        matter. To which they hiss
                        & murmur & mess when I hold
                        something as simple & delicate

                        as asking a friend
                        if it were meant
                                            :: to be ::

that somehow could we still share   *:: time ::*   all the while with *Efes* passing through

me & has been
& relentlessly
reaching & reaching for
& sometimes touching

God—

& still you stand at the same river,

thinking of the answer you gave, one from where the head

cannot meet the heart

for reasons unknown.

EFES WRESTLING WITH THE POET WHO WON'T LOOK AWAY

To set fire to warships in the water   cast your mirror

as parabola. You still won't quiet these waters.   Finite are bodies

to drown. Infinite only the quarks & electrons that you won't see   keeping

you as one. As more than. Similar. *Don't reduce me*, says the reflection. But it's already done.

It's a whisper. As if nothing still. Lies outside Saturn & Jupiter. Vibrating the highest key &

timbre:: timber. Only in time is your God. Safe. In song smeared by a warhero across my zero

believers. They never give up. You, poet, are more than. Similar to this. Terror. In clear water

the nautilus forgets easily. After a day it swims again straight toward me. Hungering. & you

hold a single knife. Without one fundamental sliver. Or steady. Particle. I will always. Terrify

water into flame. Devour shell & cirrus. Ornate & plain. This is giving myself. As. Ghosting.

Timelines. & entrapment. What comes after an entrance. & harmony. Drowns you in sleep.

POET WRESTLING WITH THE POETICS OF UNSOLVABLE PHYSICS

Maybe I *am* writing this   to get you   to stop
pursuing me,   my little vampire bunny—   & maybe

     these questions aren't meant   to be
     solved.   Maybe they are playing

  you & me   like a fork a little too sharply
  tuned.   Is the true   nature of Dark Energy.

     Being a little off   is the right kind
     of beacon.   For eternity.

       Owes everything   to lust,

        the cruelest kind
         of swelling that cannot *release* {release}

    & will always cost
      any kind of future
        {worth remembering}.

Maybe I am. Writing this for you, my sweet, sweet.
But I'm lost. In a bigger thicket of grit   & greed

     wanting more   of itself,   *just a second longer*? Do you ever think

       that's why you're always hungry.   & those love bites   aren't so
       tender.   & whatever.   Force drives you   {to spring upon me}

doesn't yet exist.   It's
okay.   To say *well, nothing*

would change   ::you::   {*would still. Love me.*}   I don't
mind,   the attempts   to fertilize   immortality.

But does perfect pitch lead anywhere   &   beyond {*closing
a circle*}?   Like tying intricate knot   without purpose?

But go on. & anyway. Bind   my legs & arms   in your infinite   & immaculate
vampire bunny   charms. & gravity   of desire.   Isn't an eternal light   left alone

in perfection   a life gone   stale.   I'm betting & only on
defects. & kinks.   As what moves anything.   Forward.   No,

it's not light. Or reaching.
        Apex—not the kind of animal
                you pretend   to reconcile.
                        I know the living dead are real.

Every time you kill me.
        To prove my protons
                Are. Fundamentally stable. Talk is cheap.
                        As it is small. I'd rather take {*chance*} & get

gnawed. & chewed & chomped
& become delicious & seduced
as. Evolution. Is.   Seriously

screwed.   Since questions
seek {*out*} their own
silencing.

Is that why you bite me {*dead*},
my little bunny—to turn us
into peculiar
velocity?

Your quantum features seek   my gravity. & maybe
infinitely   cottontail & fangs   caught *on*

doorways   because Dark Energy says we   shouldn't?
What *multiplies* when yet still. I arise   from torn fur & nails

digging? Maybe it were. *Big Bounce* more than.   *Big Bang*.

Maybe dry veins
nibble. & one more night
we're still bloody peas.
& quarks.
& maybe it's not important.
To the Theory of Everything,

but even after they come for you,

I keep & keep. Seeing. & everywhere,
my sweet little bloodsucking.
How you appear, suddenly,
on trains

popping out of cat carriers & staring
from screened windowsill.
Is that not you purring

at the diner when they serve you up medium-
rare on gilded plate.   *Skunned* & still

bloody. Steam
rising

from the toothpick they speared
into your twitching,
cold heart
& I tear

onto, my tears like the problem
of {capital T} Theory & my ears
like {capital E} Everything.   Is

it all over the moment
one gets just close enough
to what is Ultimate
& Final—

is that when Everything is proven. Fatal.   Because such proximity
does not lead to anything more
than little vampire bunnies
who were just as human
as the last question
I will eat from my own
swollen & stained lips.

{POST} :: LUDE

You mean more to me than any scientific truth.

—*SOLARIS* (1972)

POET WRESTLING WITH REVERSE {RE-VERSE} STRING THEORY

What if we are the science
fiction.   Or the humors

of Dark Energy.   Who will always be stronger. & who
the diction.   To gain influence & power.   & encrypted {*I*

          see you}.   &   I have so many questions

               for You :: with{out} You :: of You [searching]

                    for another. Planet. To {re}
                    -*descent*. Take a listen. Take
                    rest. It's so tiring. I'm *tiring*

     of Your constant & intrinsic

       invisibility.

     I crave   {I see You, *Efes*}

not hiding but {in} wait.   *Efesito mio.* My dulce & little   {*I will reduce*}

   unlike anything

     nullifies not unlike—   I agree

with the dreamers. & dancers & healers {*without you*}. With viruses & needful
   disease—   all those visionaries who make up a multiverse

of quivering little strings.

Even if they aren't   :: all :: {of Your} singing   {*without*

You [I'm strung out with]}   & trembling.

If something doesn't sing, then it is not real
until You are

EVERYWHERE & WILL NOT DIE

:: in theory ::

Take a rest. I'm tiring. Of time
{*without you*}   & matter

—

{*I will bend you & backwards   & bang & boom—*}

Patience. Partner

particles [404 Error] {*un
-founded*} lest a—

{*higher energy—*}

Patience.

Carry this {*out*}.
You are to me
so unknowingly. What
reveals. A begetting most

{*—un-naturally*}

*

I suspect.   *Efes.*   That You are the one. Breaking.   Our {*tinpot bolts & springs*} Theory

of Everything.

& how elegance is very.   & very wrong.
To trick us.   Into seducing. Gravity.

Only You. Flex.   {*The Light*}.
Against. & into. All
these little strings. I   suspect.

                              Dark Energy is the result of *Efes*.
                              Having Its way.

I am singing: Dark Energy is the result of You having Your way.

Maiming every charge & spin
as we ever & only know them.   Tempting us.   To

                                        {*jump, jump*—}

              Hallo. New. Zero {*-Point*}
              World. How will You end
              me now. What will
              You almost give. Just.
              To {with}hold one. & last
                  ungracious bow?

*

Hallo I'm pretty sure   my God   thinks I've lost
my way   when I sing   my ears {*are*} full

of Dark Energy Efes

                        & all these planets
running away. Our universe
on the run. & savage.

I {have} run away too {Most of my—}
Found in foreclosed. Alleys. Up.
{*Thunderstruck.*} Trees. Attics. Dunes.
Boneyards. The Sinai. Lost time.
Down. Cliff. &. Motorcycle—

Someone I could never see
calls. My begetters. It was You
who'd answer. Dust in thicket. Most
punishing of our truss. I never knew

my fate that night. Any {*sand-*}
storm & broken branch. When
exactly my heart   would end

waiting for You. *Hallo.*   I'm pretty
maimed. & the shaming of. Asking.
What was wrong. Did You ever care.

To know the secrets. I possess.
What time I {*ran with*}
a sharing of darkness.

You have all. Your answers {*the*

night}. There's no room.

To escape. & You.

Know that none.

Can hold

me   {*I'm bending bars & singing electric   third rails—*}

—I boast in Efes voice: *I'd like to bend a lot more than spacetime.*

                                                    {I'm growing

                          wandering black holes in my eyes   they vibrate   ::   *like drowning}*

You want to be the greatest nothing

        never told

            in full :: You want

an ever-expanding distance between us

            :: collapse each & every

                world until we are gone ^{in You}

                    {& without you}

*

To tell ^{ItAll} :: to sense ^{some}

      {to fabric{ate} :: to populate

            & pluck   starhorses

                              on broken stringed lyre}

This is a year in my life of eroded energies   & nerves of misfire

I spin & spin   a twisting neuron :: You spin {in} dimensions

               {*I'll never exist*}

You strike in elevator   music   & burned
rubber nearly missing   a red light You hiss

in gulls off abuelo's rickety boat my tattered
sundress as tattered as storm-tossed shore

       & wanton seaweed & wanton jellyfish {I
           let} sting me without
       seeing You come to me at holy
       wall of a temple long gone
       eating the prayer I stuck
       between the stone

       when I prayed in finite direction   & lived solitary
       among my people   my people all around
       I could not no longer   hear   God

{*was it you*} was it You ^{withoutYou}

coming to me in ports of call & gates teeming with delays
      & lightning storms that ground

every single plane
      awaiting at other airports I won't leave

well enough
        & solid—

a mass in the throat of Your fate :: the fate whose second property   is mystery

        the first

            ::

              who is singing *whoest*
              who will be without stillness
              who said {auto}biography is not

                & only

      music

        of deep deep silence
        :: hyperspaceawakening ::

*

Think of a place
just like this one
in which everything

> *exists*
> *as it is*
> *& should be*

> > *except you*
> > *are not*
> > *there—*

one where your God only gives The Light

> > *& another where I {am complete &} nullify—*

> > > unlike here, where You

> are the reason why
> we are just unstable enough
> for 11 dimensions. Why 1::1

> > a fate
> > given
> > & not
> > shared,

where One is my God

& One is the growing

power of

Isn't.

*

It's like this: If I die ::   I'll give birth to something   ::: to nullify.

I *promise*. I'm partial to smacking
     galactic dust
     across bared
     chests & broad
     measures that reduce

     my words to subatomic membranes
     that croon much, much
     more
                       fatally.

*

Say Isn't could be. *Everything.*

Take our 11 dimensional. Multiverse.

I. Say: *Make more*. Because why stop there I know

> I wouldn't
> & I'm just one
> body or set of rules
> I break in a heartbeat
> for a feeling
> of thrill
> *wreckless*
> *wreckless*   am
> I another long long trick
> of existence   still burning
>
> like a halogen
>   -lit hot
> plate I leave on after the fire burns
> an entire world   & mass
> burial is the only possible
> memory   taken
> & annulled

> > {*Efes   teeming through me*
> > *beyond electric*   I feel
> >
> > smaller things
> > than neutrinos}

I will love You impossible 12th dimension

I will love You irascibly   & irresistibly *hard*

I will You love You enough to question

why the others think they know numbers {*those worlds*

entire—} & how each behaves {*always so perfectly*}

If anyone were to say *I* was *their* idea

of {one}   I'd immediately

split into 1::1

                    + 11

                              + 1 & burst

                                             into choking
                                             ecstatic little strings

          O I'd take breath away
          as 12th dimension &   *skun* flesh
          to increase for pleasure   of the sudden
          last gasp there would be not time for them   to draw {in}

I'd end   singing them   to sleep with all my little

vibrations & still   would it be   more simple~yes~

Than it is^{yes}
For you{*yes*}
To exist*yes*
As nullification   *yes*

*

Nothing's as simple as saying a vampire bunny thumps & grinds

His fangs only when something much worse is coming for those dead

Eyes red & wide when it's a case of mistaken identity {*I see You Efes*} I'm onto

You the thumping is in control of the bunny & the undead bunny's destiny

Of forces yet unnamed I get it that You desire me as You desire

All things   though   I can bind & clinch   my vibrations

Stronger   let him drain me   choke   {on} lesser eternities

I won't let it undead me or ask for one more day no

I won't ask for mercy just

One more

Kiss

*

& if You remain *unfounded* is it

              a death

                       that ends not too :: with us

& if I jam Your projections

            hot & dense
            graffitied on
            falling fence

                     would You last known
                     survivor swim upside
                     -down through worm-
                     hole &   come face-
                     to-face with Your other
                     half Absolute
                             & Perfected

How long You must be   & weary of Each

      Other & seeking   hope

   & sorrow & sanctity within

               :: {*burning*} :: me

                     doubtful
          & aching

endless   tunnel

of ecstasy

not yet reaching One

Another

I have been pulled in many directions & dragged along
invisible bridgings   .   without one last road only

more long & annular vibrations
that will not close
nor circle

back. Do You hear how. You Each sing this through.
Me. & I sing too. Transmission :: Creator.   Love{r}

:: Void. It's 3:25 am on the second day of Sep-
tember. I won't press {enter} to finish the last

word. I will remember this day. What it takes to. Re-
verse the last of waning quasar. Singing promises of

new stars I chose. Love over proof. Of witness. To-
morrow will come as. I'm hot & dense & pulsating

without predictions   :: *Your longing*   *of long dances* ::
opening Your mouth for the first time   I was the opposite

side   a 4-dimensional bridge torn   & trembling

the voice of my God
Your unspoken Twin
who too was not
alone
in self-

        suspicions   did We all not trip

                        The Light together   *:: enjambed ::*

        wreckless &
        ramshackle
        threads   *binded*
        & {unsounding}   in un-
        equal doubt &
        immeasurable   dread how
        even numbers are nothing
        promised nor
        blessed

when You final

                  -ly touch

      One Another   &

    rip

                  right through me—

will I be   still
there   & already

a little too
       :: *late* ::

     & losing

       light that will
       not escape

when I no longer {*have*}
matter

   :: vision ultra-
     violet & infra-
      red will You not

see me then
without end

a :: other side

   a sea
   endlessly
  :: spinning ::

I drift upon what last
words   {I} won't

: :: sling-

{*shot*} faulty & error :: :

was it :: {*in would be*} :: ever :: real

is there {am next} & will we

:: *sing* ::

{*o perhaps You*
& You & I
will until
something

:: *Greater than* ::

gives—}

o o o what if

{*what if*}

ACKNOWLEDGMENTS & NOTES

Grateful acknowledgment is made to the editors of the following journals in which these poems first appeared, some in different form or with different titles: *The Common*, *Cordite Poetry Review* (Australia), *FIVE:2:ONE*, *Guernica*, *Glass: A Journal of Poetry*, *Hobart*, *Hunger Mountain*, *The Journal*, *Mississippi Review*, *Poetry*, *The Poetry Review* (UK), *Poets of Queens* (Anthology), *The Puritan* (Canada), *The Rumpus*, *Salamander*, *Shrew*, *The Shallow Ends*, & *Waxwing*.

A graviton is the theoretical force particle of gravity, which has a mass of zero & has not yet been experimentally proven.

"Poet Wrestling with Derelict Spacecraft" references a particular question asked in *Sefer Yetzirah* (Book of Formation) that distinguishes zero from all other numbers: "Before one, what do you count?" It also references the Chassidic idea of "Three Heads of the Crown:" אֶפֶס —*Efes*, which means "to nullify" or "to conceal" & the highest head (*Radla*); ע —Ayin, the sixteenth letter in the Hebrew *Alefbet*, which means "nothingness"; & תֹהוּ —*Tohu*, which means "Chaos."

*

So much love to my family, my parents & my Uncle George & Aunt Mary Gomez who spent one rainy October evening in the Rio Grande Valley listening to these weird wirings & zero-point energy dreams of a better world. To Stacey Pisarczyk for jumping on a train when my own wiring first went faulty in my body almost a decade ago. To all the Gomez fam. To Ben (whose jokes are still just kinda funny), Julie & Rachel. To Bakar, Robin & Cheri. To Brian, Goose & our once-family.

Many thanks & much love to Diane Chang & Clint Guthrie & Ellison Dove, Darrel Alejandro Holnes, Dorothy Chan, Holly Burdorff, Ruben Quesada, Jasminne & Lupe Mendez, Gabby Bellot, Aimee, Scott, Jackson & Hunter Coleman, Jason Koo, Joe & Wendy Pan, Lynn Melnick, Kirsten Reach,

R.A. Villanueva, Roberto Carlos Garcia, Yesenia Montilla, Menelle Sebastien, Carolina Ebeid, Becca Klaver, Nomi Stone & Jared Harél who read or heard earlier versions of these poems, as it manifested in all its *Efesito* ways.

Much love to Chef Tim & his staff at Quaint, which is one of the best restaurants in New York City, & that's where we went the night I found out this book won the Alice James Award. & the wonderful people at TJ Asian Bistro & SoleLuna where I talked through many of these poems in that much very beloved stretch of Queens.

Billions & billions of Dark-Energy-level love to Alice James, for taking on this book. This is one of the happiest moments in my life.

"The Songs We Know Not to Talk Over" is in loving memory of my Uncle Julian "Balani" Gomez the II and my Aunt Olivia Cisneros.

"Poet Wrestling with the Day the Sun Stood Still in Cold November Rain" is for Aimee & Scott Coleman.

"If This Is the Age We End Discovery" is for Aimee Nezhukumatathil, after her poem "Chess."

"Poet Wrestling with *Rick and Morty* but Mostly Rick" is after *Rick and Morty*.

RECENT TITLES FROM ALICE JAMES BOOKS

ALICE JAMES BOOKS is committed to publishing books that matter. The press was founded in 1973 in Boston, Massachusetts as a cooperative, wherein authors performed the day-to-day undertakings of the press. This element remains present today, as authors who publish with the press are invited to collaborate closely in the publication process of their work. AJB remains committed to its founders' original feminist mission, while expanding upon the scope to include all voices and poets who might otherwise go unheard. In keeping with its efforts to build equity and increase inclusivity in publishing and the literary arts, AJB seeks out poets whose writing possesses the range, depth, and ability to cultivate empathy in our world and to dynamically push against silence. The press was named for Alice James, sister to William and Henry, whose extraordinary gift for writing went unrecognized during her lifetime.

Designed by Alban Fischer

Printed by McNaughton & Gunn